The Making of Everyday Things

Books

Derek Miller

New York

Published in 2020 by Cavendish Square Publishing, LLC
243 5th Avenue, Suite 136, New York, NY 10016

Copyright © 2020 by Cavendish Square Publishing, LLC

First Edition

No part of this publication may be reproduced, stored in a retrieval system, or transmitted in any form or by any means—electronic, mechanical, photocopying, recording, or otherwise—without the prior permission of the copyright owner. Request for permission should be addressed to Permissions, Cavendish Square Publishing, 243 5th Avenue, Suite 136, New York, NY 10016. Tel (877) 980-4450; fax (877) 980-4454.

Website: cavendishsq.com

This publication represents the opinions and views of the author based on his or her personal experience, knowledge, and research. The information in this book serves as a general guide only. The author and publisher have used their best efforts in preparing this book and disclaim liability rising directly or indirectly from the use and application of this book.

All websites were available and accurate when this book was sent to press.

Library of Congress Cataloging-in-Publication Data

Names: Miller, Derek L., author.
Title: Books / Derek Miller.
Description: First edition. | New York : Cavendish Square, 2020. | Series: The making of everyday things | Includes index.
Identifiers: LCCN 2018052351 (print) | LCCN 2018060247 (ebook) | ISBN 9781502647047 (ebook) | ISBN 9781502647030 (library bound) | ISBN 9781502647023 (pbk.) | ISBN 9781502647054 (6 pack)
Subjects: LCSH: Books--Juvenile literature. | Book industries and trade--Juvenile literature.
Classification: LCC Z116.A2 (ebook) | LCC Z116.A2 M48 2020 (print) | DDC 002--dc23
LC record available at https://lccn.loc.gov/2018052351

Editorial Director: David McNamara
Copy Editor: Nathan Heidelberger
Associate Art Director: Alan Sliwinski
Designer: Ginny Kemmerer
Production Coordinator: Karol Szymczuk
Photo Research: J8 Media

The photographs in this book are used by permission and through the courtesy of: TK

Printed in the United States of America

Contents

Books **4**

New Words **22**

Index **23**

About the Author **24**

Books are fun!

They also help us learn.

They have many parts.

Making a book is a lot of work!

Pages are made of paper.

Paper is thin.

Books can have many thin pages.

7

Pages start as big rolls of paper.

The rolls are huge!

One roll makes many pages.

9

A **printer** uses **ink** to add words to the paper.

Ink is colored.

It is easy to read on the white paper.

There are different kinds of printers.

Some are very big.

They print many pages at a time.

The big sheets of paper are cut.

Now they are pages.

But the pages are not in order.

The pages need **collating**.

Collating is putting them in order.

A machine collates the pages.

The book cover is thick white paper.

Color is printed on it.

The pages are **bound**.

They are glued into the cover.

The cover **protects** the pages.

The book is ready to read!

It was not easy to make.

But now people can enjoy it.

21

New Words

bound (BOWND) Stuck together.

collating (KOH-late-ing) Putting pages in order.

ink (INK) A colored liquid used to print words.

printer (PRIN-ter) A machine that puts ink on paper.

protects (pruh-TEHKTS) Keeps safe.

Index

bound, 18

collating, 16

cover, 18, 20

cut, 14

ink, 10

order, 14, 16

paper, 6, 8, 10, 14, 18

printer, 10, 12

protects, 20

rolls, 8

About the Author

Derek Miller is a teacher and writer. He likes to learn interesting facts about things we see every day.

About

Bookworms help independent readers gain reading confidence through high-frequency words, simple sentences, and strong picture/text support. Each book explores a concept that helps children relate what they read to the world they live in.